Boots On The Ground
Taking the first steps toward ekklesia

Published by
Kingdom Word Publications
Albion, Michigan 49224
Printed in the USA

Boots On The Ground
Taking the first steps toward ekklesia

Copyright © 2025 by T. Lemoss Kurtz
All Rights Reserved

ISBN 9781735852690
Library of Congress Control Number: 2025905141

Unless otherwise noted, all scripture references are taken from the New King James Version of the Bible. No portion of this book may be reproduced, stored in a retrieval system, or transmitted in any form of by any means, electronic, mechanical photocopy, recording, or any other means except for brief quotations in printed reviews, with the prior written permission of the publisher.

When appropriate, scriptural references with the word church have been changed to ekklesia.

All references to satan and the devil are not capitalized in this book, even when it is literally proper to do so.

Kingdom Word Publications is the publishing division of The Ekklesia Center and Ekklesia Center Ministries. The mission of Kingdom Word Publications is to produce and distribute quality books and training materials to strengthen believers who are gathering from house to house, according to the values and structure of first century Christianity.

For more information, visit our website www.TheEkklesiaCenter.org

Table of Contents

	Introduction	i
Chapter 1:	Ekklesia: Embracing A Paradigm Shift	1
Chapter 2:	Ekklesia: What Must Be Done On Earth	9
Chapter 3:	Boots On The Ground: Equipping Believers To Advance The Kingdom	17
Chapter 4:	Taking The Word Everywhere	25
Chapter 5:	You Are Qualified	37
Chapter 6:	Established, Developed, and Released	47
Chapter 7:	Let's Get Started	57
	How To Start A Home or Small Group Gathering	79
	Recommendation for How To Receive the Lord's Table in a Home or Small Group Gathering	85

Dedicated to the emerging army of
Kingdom Citizens who know they are
called out to serve in the ekklesia

INTRODUCTION

I never quite understood how I became part of the collaborative team that helped shape the direction of the Global Kingdom Conversation (GKC). It remains a mystery to me. But what I do know is that it was an incredible honor—one that I continue to treasure to this day. It was within that space that *Boots on the Ground* was born.

The GKC met weekly on Zoom, drawing men and women from several nations. Each session was filled with rich discussions on a variety of topics, all centered around guiding those who sought to embrace what God was doing in this season. At the time, I was bi-vocational—balancing a secular job while leading a ministry. Because of my work schedule, I couldn't always attend the live sessions in full. Sometimes, I could only catch fragments.

One afternoon, I logged in late and was surprised to hear my name mentioned. The discussion had turned to my teachings on *ekklesia,* and to my astonishment, it was being announced that I was being requested to present to the GKC on the topic.

I was honored, but I also knew I didn't have the full picture. There was another voice that needed to be included. A brother from Nigeria, Temidayo 'Dayo' Adeyemo. He and I had connected through our shared passion for ekklesia. I reached out to Dayo regarding the presentation, and he agreed to take part.

Later that week, we were only able to schedule one brief meeting to discuss the presentation. In our conversation, we both recognized a common issue—there was a lot of dialogue about ekklesia, but very little action. Today, neither of us can recall exactly who first said the phrase *Boots on the Ground,* but we immediately agreed on its significance. Ekklesia had to move beyond articulation into activation.

On February 3, 2023, 'Dayo' and I presented *Church & Ekklesia: Boots on the Ground* to the GKC. Neither of us knew in advance what the other would say, but when it was over, we both realized something powerful had taken place. The outcome exceeded our expectations.

That presentation became the genesis of this book you now hold in your hands. *Boots on the Ground* is more than a concept—it is a call to action.

You can listen to the full presentation here: https://youtu.be/T-GaDrNK21k?si=y_AMKm2o7D_L4zSl

FAST FORWARD TWO YEARS

Since that day Dayo and I presented *Church & Ekklesia: Boots on the Ground* to the Global Kingdom Conversation, the concept has never left my spirit. What started as a phrase in a discussion has become a defining pathway—one that leads from where we are to where we should be.

My book, *Leaving Church, Becoming Ekklesia*, was written to help believers transition from the church system to the ekklesia Jesus said He would build. But over the years, I've come to see just how deeply the traditional church structure has held many in religious bondage.

I've spoken to countless believers who sense there's more to their faith than the weekly cycle of Sunday services. Many have confided in me about what they believe God has called them to do, yet they struggle to find an outlet to walk it out. I've counseled those who, out of frustration, wanted to leave their church altogether. To them, I always gave the same advice: don't leave out of anger—seek the Lord for direction. I do not advocate rebellion, but I also know that staying within the confines of a system that suppresses one's spiritual growth can be just as damaging.

At the same time, I heard pastors telling their congregations, "*You need a pastor and a church home*", as though without them, believers are spiritually deficient. Meanwhile, I was teaching about ekklesia—a concept that many found difficult to grasp and even harder to live out in any tangible way.

Over time, I began to see *Boots on the Ground* as more than just a phrase—it was an entry point. It could serve as a bridge for those who were sensing the call to something greater but didn't know how to take the first step. It could be the missing link between leaving behind the limitations of church-as-we-know-it and stepping fully into the ekklesia Jesus is building.

Even with the challenges that may come with such a shift, the idea excites me.

It is critical that accurate teaching on ekklesia continues. For over six years, I provided daily insights on the subject, producing over 600 videos on my YouTube channel. Then, in October of 2023, the Lord gave me clear instruction to shut down my daily broadcast, *Good Morning, Ekklesia*. As much as I loved doing those teachings, I understood why He was leading me to close that chapter. He showed me that while many were being informed about ekklesia, they weren't being transformed by it. They were consuming the teaching but not activating it. That had to change.

The world is in turmoil. Economic instability, racial and social divides, political corruption, and environmental crises plague nearly every nation. Yet, in the midst of it all, this is the season when the Lord is bringing His ekklesia to the forefront. He is calling out believers—those who are ready to engage the issues of our time with a *'thy Kingdom come, thy will be done on earth'* mindset.

This book will outline the *Boots on the Ground* mission to expand the kingdom through believers like you. My prayer is that it will provide a clear biblical pathway for you to step into what God has called you to be in this season. Jesus is still building His ekklesia, and He's doing it through believers like you.

Blessings,

Tim Kurtz
March 2025

1
EKKLESIA:
EMBRACING A PARADIGM SHIFT

Little did I know that two books, *Beyond Church: The Lost Word of the Bible*[1] and *Ekklesia Rising: The Authority of Christ in Communities of Contending Prayer*[2], would have such a profound impact on me.

These books came at a time when I was searching for direction. I was trying to write a sequel to my book, *No Longer Church As Usual: Restoring First Century Values and Structure to the 21st Century Church.*[3] Nothing I

---

[1] BEYOND CHURCH: *the lost word of the bible* © 2015 by Steve Simms, Published by Harper Simms Press

[2] EKKLESIA RISING: *The Authority of Christ in Communities of Contending Prayer* © 2014 by Dean Briggs, Published by Champion Press, Kansas City, MO

[3] NO LONGER CHURCH AS USUAL: *Restoring First Century Values and Structure to the 21st Century Church* © 2010 by T. Lemoss Kurtz, Second Edition ©2013 by T. Lemoss Kurtz, Published by Kingdom Word Publications

attempted to write made sense until I was presented with these two books that introduced me to ekklesia.

To be clear, I was familiar with ekklesia but had assumed like many that it was the Greek word that was translated into English as church. These books thrust me into a new understanding, as well as a powerful shift in what Jesus intended when He declared He would build His ekklesia – not church.

The more I explored ekklesia—historically, etymologically, and biblically—the more I realized that something was misaligned with how we were practicing our faith.

What I discovered wasn't a matter of salvation. Many of those around me genuinely loved the Lord and served Him wholeheartedly, according to their understanding. However, I began to see a stark difference between how we functioned and what was revealed in Scripture. The deeper purpose behind our faith seemed either greatly diminished or entirely absent.

Unfortunately, many believers were—and still are—unaware of this missing piece. For most, the ultimate goal is simply to get to heaven, while others are primarily focused on the rapture. Yet, as I read certain passages of Scripture, I found that these perspectives didn't fully align with what Jesus taught.

Let's examine the biblical account of when Jesus first introduced ekklesia.

> *When Jesus came into the region of Caesarea Philippi, He asked His disciples, saying, "Who do men say that I, the Son of Man, am?" So they said, "Some say John the Baptist, some Elijah, and others Jeremiah or one of the prophets." He said to them, "But who do you say that I am?" Simon Peter answered and said, "You are the Christ, the Son of the living God." Jesus answered and said to him, "Blessed are you, Simon Bar-Jonah, for flesh and blood has not revealed this to you, but My Father who is in heaven. "And I also say to you that you are Peter, and on this rock I will build My [ekklesia] and the gates of Hades shall not prevail against it. (Matthew 16:13-18 – ekklesia added for clarification)*

Caesarea Philippi was no ordinary place. It was oozing with idolatry. It was brazenly occultic. It was visibly filthy. And, it was home to many pagan activities. Yet, it was there that Jesus chose to solidify His revelatory identity with His disciples. Keep in mind, they had traveled nearly twenty miles out of the way to this place to have Jesus ask them, "Who do men say that I am?" followed by, "Who do you say that I am?" Of course, we know that Peter blurted out, "You are the Christ, Son of the Living God!" It was from this that Jesus declared He would build His ekklesia. I want to be abundantly clear that Jesus did not imply, suggest, or infer anything close to the English word church.

I found myself wondering—why would Jesus choose such a forbidden place to ask His disciples about His true identity? Why is a deep, revelatory understanding of who He is essential for Him to build His ekklesia? And what exactly was an ekklesia, and why did Jesus choose to establish His version of it? When Jesus said that the 'gates of Hades' would not prevail against His ekklesia, it was obvious that some level of conflict was on the horizon. As I continued reading, it became increasingly clear that Jesus was on a deliberate mission.

> *"And I will give you the keys of the kingdom of heaven, and whatever you bind on earth will be bound in heaven, and whatever you loose on earth will be loosed in heaven." Then He commanded His disciples that they should tell no one that He was Jesus the Christ. (Matthew 16:19-20)*

Jesus conferred the keys of the Kingdom of Heaven to His disciples. What was most intriguing to me was that their usage was earthly – not heavenly. The keys represent full access to the resources of heaven, but those resources were to be used on earth. This shifts our focus from trying to get to heaven, to understanding our responsibility on earth. This understanding becomes the framework for Boots on the Ground.

What about the revelation that He is the Christ, Son of the Living God? Was this limited to the first apostles? Curiously, Jesus commanded His disciples not to tell anyone that He was the Christ. He wasn't restricting this truth but rather ensuring that future generations would function from divine revelation, not religious information (Galatians 1:15-16; Ephesian 1:17; 1Peter 1:13).

Scripture reveals that we were never meant to have merely an intellectual relationship with the Word. Instead, we are called to know it and live it out. What we read in Scripture is meant to be manifested in the earth.

> "*This Book of the Law shall not depart from your mouth, but you shall meditate in it day and night, <u>that you may observe to do</u> according to all that is written in it. For then you will make your way prosperous, and then you will have good success. (Joshua 1:8)*

> *<u>But be doers of the word</u>, and not hearers only, deceiving yourselves. (James 1:22)*

> "*Do you not believe that I am in the Father, and the Father in Me? The words that I speak to you I do not speak on My own authority; but the Father who dwells in Me does the works. "Believe Me that I am in the Father and the Father in*

> *Me, or else believe Me for the sake of the works themselves. "Most assuredly, I say to you, he who believes in Me, <u>the works that I do he will do also; and greater works than these he will do, because I go to My Father</u>. (John 14:10-12)*

These passages reveal a theme that cannot be ignored. We cannot be satisfied with just hearing the Word – we must be intentional about doing the Word. A word 'not done' is a wasted word. I believe every Word of God can find a place of manifestation in the earth. Allow me to show you this reality from one of my favorite passages.

> *Isaiah 55:6 Seek the LORD while He may be found, Call upon Him while He is near.*

God is not hiding from us. Yet, at times it feels like He is absent. The prophet resolves this issue by calling us to action. We are to 'seek the Lord' while He may be found. Again, this is not because He is hiding, but rather that we have lost sight of Him. Once you sense you are in the vicinity of where He is, call on Him. Don't hold back. Don't let others discourage or distract you. Call Him. He is ready to answer (Mark 10:46-52).

> *Isaiah 55:7 Let the wicked forsake his way, and the unrighteous man his thoughts: and let him return unto the LORD,*

> *and he will have mercy upon him; and to our God, for he will abundantly pardon.*

In His presence, make whatever adjustments you need to make. Be willing to let go of things that hinder you. Change your way of thinking to align with Him. Live with expectancy of His mercy.

> *Isaiah 55:8-9 For my thoughts are not your thoughts, neither are your ways my ways, saith the LORD. For as the heavens are higher than the earth, so are my ways higher than your ways, and my thoughts than your thoughts.*

From the time I was first saved, I often heard people quote these two verses with a sigh of religious resignation, implying that God's ways and thoughts are so far beyond us that we can never understand them. While it is true that His ways and thoughts are much higher than ours, He graciously reveals them to us through His Word and by revelation. The truth is, God wants us to know His thoughts and ways. The next verses prove it.

> *Isaiah 55:10-11 For as the rain cometh down, and the snow from heaven, and returneth not thither, but watereth the earth, and maketh it bring forth and bud, that it may give seed to the sower, and bread to the eater: So shall my word be that goeth forth out of my mouth: it shall not return unto*

> *me void, but it shall accomplish that which I please, and it shall prosper in the thing whereto I sent it.*

Take a moment to consider the powerful picture of rain and snow and how they change the earth. They constantly nourish the soil, making it thrive and produce food for those who plant seeds. The prophet uses this vivid example to show how God's Word works in our lives. His Word holds His higher thoughts and ways, carrying His purpose and power. When He sends it out, it will never come back empty. Instead, it will always accomplish exactly what He intended.

I will discuss the next two verses in the next chapter. You will see the impact of the Word in your life. Get ready, tie your boots up. It's time to go.

2
EKKLESIA: WHAT MUST BE DONE ON EARTH

I've shown you how God's Word, filled with His higher thoughts and ways, always fulfills the purpose for which He sends it. But there's more!

"For you shall go out..."

The first sign that God's Word is alive in us is action. Too often, people quote, *"God's Word will not return to Him void,"* yet they overlook a crucial truth—*we must go!* Just like rain and snow transform the earth, making it fertile and full of life (Isaiah 55:10), God's Word is meant to activate us. When it takes root in us, it stirs movement, growth, and purpose. It's not just meant to be heard—it's meant to be done. It is sent to send us out!

> *For you shall go out with joy, and be led forth with peace: the mountains and the hills shall break forth before you into singing, and all the trees of the field shall clap their hands. Instead of the thorn shall come up the fir tree, and instead of the brier shall come up the myrtle tree: and it shall be to the LORD for a name, for an everlasting sign that shall not be cut off. (Isaiah 55:12-13)*

Something powerful happens when we step out with the Word of God—we go out with joy and are led by peace! Let me take a little scriptural liberty here and suggest that, as New Testament believers, the presence of joy and peace is a clear sign of the Holy Spirit at work in us (Acts 1:8; Romans 14:17). When we move in obedience to God's Word, we don't just carry a message—we carry His presence, His power, and His Kingdom!

But here's what excites me the most—the very atmosphere shifts as we go! Mountains and hills, which often symbolize obstacles, challenges, and worldly mindsets, won't stand in defiance; instead, they will break into song! The trees—symbolic of people and nations—will respond with joy as they encounter the move of God.

In this kind of environment, thorns—representing struggle and barrenness—can't take root. Instead, myrtle trees—symbols of life, restoration, and blessing—will flourish. This is a powerful glimpse of the ekklesia in action, transforming the earth with the unstoppable power of the Kingdom!

The key factor in this powerful transformation is 'go'. Nothing changes. Nothing is impacted. Nothing happens until you or I 'go'. This is foundational to understanding what 'Boots On The Ground' is all about. It is not about theory – it is action. To experience the reality of the high thoughts and ways of God – we must go. You will never experience the transforming power of God's Word in you until you go out with joy and peace.

GO – BUT NOT TO CHURCH

The early believers understood that they were called to bring the culture of heaven to earth (Matthew 6:10). Their mission wasn't to reflect Rome but to establish communities that embodied the values of the Kingdom—love, righteousness, peace, and justice—ultimately subverting the influence of Rome through faith.

This realization led me to a significant conclusion. When I read the narrative of Caesarea Philippi—where Jesus declared that He would build His *ekklesia*—and connected it with the original command given in the Garden of Eden (Genesis 1:28), it completely shifted my perspective.

This revelation redefined my understanding of God's purpose, showing me a continuity between His original intent for humanity and the mission of the *ekklesia* as Jesus proclaimed it.

Jesus could have said He would build His temple or synagogue. Either would have been appropriate for the religious world in the first century. Instead, He chose a secular, governmental entity whose purpose was understood by those around Him. His choice of the word ekklesia helps to shed light on His divine intent.

The Roman government used the concept of the *ekklesia* to extend and enforce its culture in conquered territories. In the Greco-Roman world, an *ekklesia* was a governing assembly made up of called-out citizens responsible for making decisions and implementing policies on behalf of the ruling authority. Rome adopted this model from the Greeks and expanded its use, transforming it into a tool for cultural and governmental influence. This allowed Rome to maintain control over its vast empire by ensuring that conquered regions aligned with its values, laws, and social structures.

When Rome took control of a new territory, it aimed to reshape it in the image of the empire. Roman laws, customs, language, and administrative systems were imposed to create a uniform identity across the empire. One of the primary ways this was accomplished was through the establishment of colonies, often populated by Roman citizens, retired soldiers, and government officials. These individuals acted as representatives of Rome, reinforcing its influence. In Roman cities, the *ekklesia* functioned as a governing body that helped manage this transition, ensuring that local populations adopted Roman ways of life and that the empire's authority remained firmly in place.

Now, think of the Roman model and consider what Jesus said He would build. He said He would build His ekklesia. The commitment was made at Caesaria Philippi. The first foundational steps were taken on the Day of Pentecost. In the two thousand plus years since, the building process has endured through attempts by the Gates of Hades to confuse, destroy, and restructure it. Here we are today in the twenty-first century standing on the advent of its full manifestation in the earth.

There is a lot of talk arising about ekklesia. There is ample confusion relating to what it is. I believe the best way to define it comes from scripture, history, and etymology. Before we can employ *Boots On The Ground*, we must be clear of our destination.

A SUMMARY OF EKKLESIA

I have given you a brief history of the Roman ekklesia. Keep in mind that this is the model Jesus chose. Thus, the expectation is that His ekklesia would emulate the same thing in behalf of the Kingdom of Heaven.

Let's be clear. Jesus said He would build His *ekklesia* – not *kuriakon*, the Greek word that would best describe church. These are two different words, with completely different meanings.

The English word 'church' did not exist in the first century. It wasn't until the seventh or eighth centuries that the word 'church' began to take form. Why is this important? If Jesus had used the English word 'church' at Caesarea Philippi, those who heard Him would have been confused. Jesus used *ekklesia* that was conceptually relevant to those He spoke to.

The transition from *ekklesia* to *church* was not a natural linguistic evolution but a deliberate mistranslation ordered by King James. The word *church* in your Bible was not divinely inspired—it was intentionally inserted to protect the king's political authority. By replacing *ekklesia*, which referred to a governing assembly of called-out believers, with *church*, which implied a religious institution, the translation reinforced the monarchy's control over Christianity.

I explore this in greater detail in Chapter Four of my book, *Leaving Church, Becoming Ekklesia*. You can download your copy of this chapter for free on my website—visit https://theekklesiacenter.org/understanding-ekklesia

As *ekklesia* gains more attention, many attempt to merge Jesus' original intent with King James' alterations. This has led to four common misconceptions:

1. <u>Ekklesia as a Church Program</u> – Some view *ekklesia* as an extension of the church, treating it as a temporary initiative or event. This makes *ekklesia* something the church can control or discard when inconvenient.

2. <u>Ekklesia as a Militant Church Movement</u> – Others see *ekklesia* as a rising force within the church, maintaining loyalty to church structures while using *ekklesia* as a platform to engage in political and social battles. This often results in political ideology being falsely presented as Kingdom authority.

3. <u>Ekklesia as Mere Semantics</u> – Some dismiss any distinction between *ekklesia* and *church*, believing the Greek term simply evolved into the modern word church. This perspective weakens the true purpose and power of *ekklesia*, reducing it to a matter of language rather than identity and function.

4. <u>Ekklesia as House Groups</u> – While I strongly support gathering from house to house, simply meeting in a

home does not fully define *ekklesia*. House gatherings are an important starting point, but *ekklesia* emerges when a group of believers is called out by the Lord to address earthly matters with Kingdom authority.

Church and ekklesia are not the same. The word church is both a mistranslation, and a misrepresentation of divine intent. It is important that you remember this as you pursue *Boots On The Ground*. Your destination is ekklesia – not church.

3
BOOTS ON THE GROUND: EQUIPPING BELIEVERS TO ADVANCE GOD'S KINGDOM

In this chapter I will give you an overview of *Boots On The Ground*. It is important that you have a basic framework for what it is and how it can work in your life.

This ministry work is for believers like you who are ready to make a tangible difference in their families, communities, cities and beyond. It's about discovering who you are in Christ, and how you matter to Him in expanding His Kingdom in the earth. It is about stepping out in faith knowing that God will use you for His glory (Acts 16:20).

BOOTS ON THE GROUND: ESTABLISHING REGIONAL EXPRESSIONS OF THE LORD'S EKKLESIA

A core objective of *Boots on the Ground* is to establish, develop, and release regional expressions of the Lord's Ekklesia by equipping believers, building connected communities, empowering individuals to make a lasting Kingdom impact, and leading people to Christ while discipling them to reach the nations. This initiative is a strategic effort to manifest God's Kingdom on earth by training and mobilizing believers to actively participate in transforming their regions through the Gospel of the Kingdom.

EQUIPPING BELIEVERS TO ACTIVELY EXPAND GOD'S KINGDOM ON EARTH THROUGH THEIR UNIQUE CALLING

Another objective of *Boots on the Ground* is to equip believers to actively engage in Kingdom expansion through their distinct callings. Every believer has been given gifts, talents, and assignments by God, and these must be nurtured and developed to fulfill the divine mandate. Equipping believers involves providing teaching, training, and mentorship to help them identify their unique role in God's plan.

The equipping process includes biblical education that emphasizes the expression of the Kingdom of God in the earth. This is done by the five-fold ministry gifts—apostles, prophets, evangelists, pastors, and teachers—as described in Ephesians 4:11-13. Each believer must discover their role within the Body of Christ and learn how to operate effectively in their calling. This involves practical training, where individuals gain hands-on experience in ministry, evangelism, and discipleship.

Moreover, equipping believers means fostering a culture of spiritual maturity. This requires teaching them how to operate in faith, discern spiritual warfare, and effectively minister to others. As individuals grow in their understanding of Kingdom principles, they become more confident and capable of expanding God's influence in their communities.

BUILDING CONNECTED COMMUNITIES OF KINGDOM CITIZENS WHO BRING TRANSFORMATION TO THEIR REGIONS WITH THE GOSPEL OF THE KINGDOM

Transformation does not happen in isolation; it requires a strong, connected community of believers working together toward a common goal. *Boots on the Ground* seeks to build such communities by fostering relationships among

Kingdom Citizens who are committed to seeing their regions transformed by the Gospel.

This begins with establishing small, home-based gatherings where believers can worship, pray, and study the Word together. These gatherings are designed to function as centers of Kingdom life, where individuals are strengthened in their faith and encouraged to live out biblical principles in their daily lives. Unlike traditional church models that emphasize centralized leadership, these gatherings operate under the headship of Christ, with believers mutually edifying and supporting one another.

Additionally, these communities must be deeply engaged in their local regions. This involves reaching out to the lost, caring for the needy, and addressing social issues from a Kingdom perspective. Whether through community service projects, evangelistic efforts, or local partnerships, these Kingdom communities aim to be the tangible expression of God's love and truth in their regions. By fostering strong relationships within and beyond the believing community, *Boots on the Ground* creates an environment where the Gospel is not only preached but lived out daily.

EMPOWERING BELIEVERS TO MAKE A LASTING KINGDOM IMPACT IN THEIR

HOMES, WORKPLACES, AND SPHERES OF INFLUENCE

The Kingdom of God is not confined to church buildings or religious gatherings; it is meant to permeate every area of life. Therefore, *Boots on the Ground* seeks to empower believers to extend God's rule and reign in their homes, workplaces, and spheres of influence. This requires a paradigm shift—moving away from a mindset that separates the sacred from the secular and embracing the understanding that every area of life is a mission field.

In the home, believers are encouraged to establish Christ-centered households where prayer, discipleship, and godly principles shape family life. Parents are equipped to raise children who understand their Kingdom identity, and marriages are strengthened through biblical guidance. When homes become places of Kingdom influence, they serve as foundational strongholds for societal transformation.

In the workplace, believers are taught to see their jobs as platforms for ministry. Whether in business, education, healthcare, or government, each individual has the opportunity to be a light in their field. Kingdom principles such as integrity, excellence, and servant leadership become defining characteristics of their professional lives. By demonstrating Christ's love and wisdom in their work environments, they create avenues for evangelism and influence.

Furthermore, believers are empowered to impact their broader spheres of influence—whether in media, arts, politics, or social activism. *Boots on the Ground* emphasizes the importance of engaging culture with the truth of the Gospel. This involves training individuals to recognize opportunities for Kingdom advancement and equipping them with strategies to bring God's righteousness, justice, and peace into every domain of society.

LEADING PEOPLE TO CHRIST, DISCIPLING THEM, AND EMPOWERING THEM TO MAKE DISCIPLES, WITH THE GOAL OF REACHING ALL NATIONS

At the heart of *Boots on the Ground* is the Great Commission—Jesus' command to make disciples of all nations (Matthew 28:18-20). This initiative is not merely about gathering believers for fellowship; it is about actively leading people to Christ and raising them up as disciples who, in turn, disciple others.

The process of disciple-making begins with evangelism. Believers are trained to share the Gospel effectively in both personal and public settings. Evangelistic efforts may include street ministry, outreach programs, digital evangelism, and relational witnessing. However, evangelism does not stop at conversion—it must be followed by intentional discipleship.

Discipleship within *Boots on the Ground* is structured to provide new believers with a strong biblical foundation. This includes teaching fundamental doctrines, fostering spiritual disciplines such as prayer and Bible study, and helping individuals develop their spiritual gifts. New believers are encouraged to grow in faith through accountability relationships and mentorship from mature Christians.

The final step in the disciple-making process is empowerment. Every disciple is trained to replicate the process by discipling others. This multiplication strategy ensures that the work of the Kingdom is continually expanding. Rather than relying on a few leaders to do the work of ministry, *Boots on the Ground* creates a movement where every believer becomes a disciple-maker, contributing to the overarching goal of reaching all nations with the Gospel.

Boots on the Ground is a Kingdom-driven initiative with a mission to establish, develop, and release regional expressions of the Lord's Ekklesia. By equipping believers, building connected communities, empowering individuals to impact their spheres of influence, and prioritizing evangelism and discipleship, this initiative seeks to advance God's Kingdom on earth.

In a world where darkness and deception seem prevalent, *Boots on the Ground* stands as a beacon of light, mobilizing believers to take an active role in transforming their regions with the truth of the Gospel. As more believers rise up to fulfill their callings and engage in the mission of disciple-making, the vision of seeing regional expressions of the Lord's Ekklesia established across the world becomes a tangible reality.

The call is clear—every believer has a role to play. The question remains: Will you put your boots on the ground and join the movement?

4
TAKING THE WORD EVERYWHERE

Jesus had been crucified, buried, and now He had risen from the dead (1Corinthians 15:3-4). For forty days after His resurrection, He preached the Kingdom, the same message He had preached throughout His ministry (Matthew 4:23; 9:35; Acts 1:1-3).

Now the disciples are gathered with Jesus one final time before He ascends back to heaven. Once they had an opportunity, the disciples asked a question regarding the restoration of the kingdom to Israel.

> "Lord, are you now restoring the kingdom to Israel?" (Acts 1:6).

Was their inquiry regarding the restoration of Israel misguided, short-sighted, or legitimate? There are several schools of thought on this subject. I reviewed several commentaries only to find an equally mixed bag of views on this matter.[1]

> And He said to them, "It is not for you to know times or seasons which the Father has put in His own authority (Acts 1:7)

It's interesting to note how Jesus responded to the disciples' question. Most commentaries agree that He did not directly rebuke or correct them for asking. However, interpretations of His response vary, which is beyond the scope of this book. I do want to highlight the JAMIESON-FAUSSET-BROWN COMMENTARY summary of Acts 1:7, as it provides an excellent bridge to what Jesus says next. It states that Jesus was *'implying not only that this was not the time, but that the question was irrelevant to their present business and future work.'*

POWER FROM THE HOLY SPIRIT

What was their present business? And, what was their future work? This was made clear in Acts 1:8 where specific

---

[1] Here are some recommended commentaries to consider on this subject: BARNES' NOTES ON THE NEW TESTAMENT, THE BIBLE KNOWLEDGE COMMENTARY, MATTHEW HENRY'S COMMENTARY ON THE WHOLE BIBLE, THE COMPLETE BIBLICAL LIBRARY: *New Testament Study Bible | Acts*; THE BIBLE EXPOSITION COMMENTARY, and the JAMIESON-FAUSSET-BROWN COMMENTARY.

marching orders for believers were given. Understanding these commands are key to *Boots On The Ground*.

> *"But you shall receive power when the Holy Spirit has come upon you; and you shall be witnesses to Me in Jerusalem, and in all Judea and Samaria, and to the end of the earth."*

Before anything else, they needed the power to carry out their assignment. That power came through the Holy Spirit. The Greek word *dunamis*, meaning miraculous and supernatural power, emphasizes the extraordinary nature of what they were called to do. This alone reveals the immense significance of their mission.

They were called to be witnesses. There are several nuances to the word witness. First, it could be a witness similar to a person in a court setting who testifies to what they personally saw (1John 1:1; 2Peter 1:16). What did they see? They personally saw the resurrected Lord, but don't lose sight of the fact that over five hundred others also saw Him (1Corinthians 15:6).

> *And that he was seen of Cephas, then of the twelve: After that, he was seen of above five hundred brethren at once; of whom the greater part remain unto this present, but some are fallen asleep. After that, he was seen of James; then of all the apostles. And last of all he was seen of me also, as of one born out of due time. (1Corinthians 15:5-8)*

Notice the order that Apostle Paul explains this.

1. Although Mary Magdelene was the first to see the resurrected Lord (Mark 16:9), among the apostles, Peter was the first to physically see Him (Luke 24:34).

2. He was then seen 'of the twelve'. This is a direct reference to the original twelve Jesus had called, of which only eleven were still alive (Mark 16:14)

3. Then Paul the Apostle stated that Jesus had been seen by more than five-hundred unnamed men.

4. AFTER THAT, He was seen of James and all the apostles. Can I suggest that the apostles mentioned here are not the original twelve. I believe these are apostles who were called and sent after Christ's ascension. I believe such apostles are being called and sent out today in the 21st Century.

5. Apostle Paul lists himself as last on the list. Remember at the time he was called and sent, he had been harshly persecuting the believers, a fact that is key to understanding *Boots On The Ground*.

The power factor cannot be ignored. It is the purpose for being a witness that triggers *Boots On The Ground*. Implicit in 1Corinthians 15:5-8, that the witnesses above were instrumental in some level of kingdom expansion. Let's look at where Jesus said they will witness.

There is a lesson to be learned from each place. I want to take you beyond the geography into the implied reason for each location.

THE WITNESS IN JERUSALEM

First, they were called to be witnesses in Jerusalem. Jerusalem is their home turf. It is a place of great familiarity. It reflects a place where you are known, and where you know many of those around you. Jerusalem is like the community where you grew up. You; your brothers, your sisters, your parents, your uncles, your aunts – are generally known. This high level of familiarity can be a hindrance to ministry. Jesus faced this very issue.

> *Then He went out from there and came to His own country, and His disciples followed Him. And when the Sabbath had come, He began to teach in the synagogue. And many hearing Him were astonished, saying, "Where did this Man get these things? And what wisdom is this which is given to Him, that such mighty works are performed by His hands! "Is this not the carpenter, the Son of Mary, and brother of James, Joses, Judas, and Simon? And are not His sisters here with us?" And they were offended at Him. But Jesus said to them, "A prophet is not without honor except in his own country, among his own relatives, and in his own*

> *house." Now He could do no mighty work there, except that He laid His hands on a few sick people and healed them. And He marveled because of their unbelief. Then He went about the villages in a circuit, teaching. (Mark 6:1-6)*

Unfortunately, many times those who know you well have a difficult time receiving anything of value from you. Even after seeing the miracles, Jesus's *'home folks'* were offended.

In the midst of this, Jesus said that, *"A prophet is not without honor except in his own country, among his own relatives, and in his own house."* I have heard ministers quote this passage to justify why they were experiencing rejection in their hometown. Yet, even as ministers, their lifestyles were shabby, questionable and unholy. They used Jesus' words as a cover against what was often justified rejection.

When witnessing in your "Jerusalem"—your hometown or a place of familiarity—it is crucial that your lifestyle reflects the holiness required by Scripture (Ephesians 5:3-5; 1Peter 4:14-16). In fact, I strongly encourage you to be especially mindful of how you live before those who know you best. Jesus understands the challenges of ministering to those in your own community. If you face rejection, let it be because of their resistance to the truth, not because of any compromise in your character. Live a life of integrity, purity, and holiness, ensuring that your actions align with the message you proclaim.

THE WITNESS IN JUDEA

The next place is Judea. Judea is where people know about you, before you know them.

> *And Jesus went about all Galilee, teaching in their synagogues, preaching the gospel of the kingdom, and healing all kinds of sickness and all kinds of disease among the people. <u>Then His fame went throughout all Syria</u>; and they brought to Him all sick people who were afflicted with various diseases and torments, and those who were demon-possessed, epileptics, and paralytics; and He healed them. Great <u>multitudes followed Him--from Galilee, and from Decapolis, Jerusalem, Judea,</u> and beyond the Jordan. (Matthew 4:23-25)*

Admittedly, marketing has never been my strength. I often hear people say that I should do more to sell my books and promote my teachings about ekklesia. I appreciate their concern, and I am deeply confident in what I teach and grateful for the books I have written. Yet, I continually ask myself, *"What is the proper way to get the word out?"*

Jesus devoted Himself to doing the will of the Father, and as a result, His fame spread organically throughout the regions (Mark 1:26-28; 3:7-8; Luke 4:14). He did not rely on self-promotion, yet His works and His life testified of Him wherever He went.

Is it wrong to promote what you do? No. However, it becomes dangerous when more effort is spent crafting an image rather than producing genuine fruit. Many have built religious platforms that appear powerful and 'anointed' on the surface, yet their lives tell a different story, one that is grossly unbiblical.

When Jesus sends us to our 'Judea,' we should be known by two things: *our documented fruit and the report of our holy living* (1Timothy 3:7; 3John 12). Our reputation should not be based on marketing tactics alone but on a consistent testimony of integrity, faithfulness, and the undeniable evidence of a life transformed by Christ. Marketing may help spread a message, but it is a life well-lived that carries the true weight of influence.

THE WITNESS IN SAMARIA

The third place we must learn to witness is in Samaria. Keep in mind that Jesus was instructing His young Jewish disciples. Jerusalem and Judea have their challenges, but now you need to go into Samaria?

There were centuries of animosity embedded between the Jews and the Samaritans. These grew from religious corruption and intermarriage that resulted in mixing pagan rituals into the worship of God (2Kings 17:24-29). Resentment remained from the Samaritans attempt to thwart the rebuilding of the temple (Ezra 4:1-5; Nehemiah 4:1-2). One of the most bitter points of contention was the rejection of the temple in Jerusalem by the Samaritans. The background for this was recorded by Flavius Josephus, a first century historian where he records how Sanballat was instrumental in erecting an alternate temple on Mount Gerizim.[2]

Bible historians believe that it was Mount Gerizim that the Samaritan woman at the well was referring to (John 4:20). No doubt this was part of the reason she was taken aback by Jesus's willingness to interact with her (John 4:9). I'm sure the disciples had some questions of their own (John 4:27).

So why Samaria? Samaria represents the people who you don't like, as much as they don't like you. They are the people you would rather avoid than interact with. Yet, Jesus said we are to be witnesses among them. If you fail among them, I believe you disqualify yourself from being effectively used further. Your Samaria is the last step

---

[2] THE WORKS OF JOSEPHUS *Complete and Unabridged* translated by William Whiston: Page 242 Antiquities of the Jews Book 11, Chapter 8, Section 2

before you are capable of going to the uttermost parts of the earth.

WITNESS IN THE UTTERMOST PARTS OF THE EARTH

Yes, the final place we are to be witnesses is 'the uttermost parts of the earth'.

In over three decades of ministry, I have encountered numerous ministers who have their sights on 'world-wide ministry' endeavors. To attempt to reach the world is admirable, but to do so being ill-equipped is both dangerous and damaging.

Paul understood that his ministry assignment was unique and carried a distinct purpose. Aware of the importance of accountability, he submitted himself to "those of reputation" to confirm that the message he preached to the Gentiles was both sound and affirmed (Galatians 2:2). This act of submission not only validated his teaching but also fortified his authority in ministry.

Yet, Paul's greatest challenge came from those who opposed him—the religious leaders who should have recognized the truth he carried. These adversaries became his *Samaria*—the place of resistance that tested and refined his message. Just as Jesus declared that the gospel would be preached in *Jerusalem, Judea, Samaria, and to the ends of the earth* (Acts 1:8), Paul's ability to stand firm among his critics ensured that his message carried the strength to reach everywhere.

Despite rejection, Paul ministered boldly. When the disciples initially doubted his conversion, Barnabas vouched for him, leading to his acceptance (Acts 9:26-27). In Thessalonica, he faced hostility from jealous religious leaders, yet he continued to preach (Acts 17:5-7). In Jerusalem, he skillfully used the theological divide between the Pharisees and Sadducees to defend himself (Acts 23:6-10). His unwavering commitment demonstrated that the gospel, once proven in opposition, could thrive anywhere.

Paul's journey teaches us that resistance is not a sign of failure but a proving ground. By facing his *Samaria*, he ensured that his message was unshakable, ready to transform not only the receptive but also those who resisted.

WHERE ARE YOU?

The Lord is calling His people to impact the earth, but He will not bypass His divine order in sending them out. Before stepping forward, take a moment to assess where you are on this journey.

Are you in your *Jerusalem*? Do you need to address areas in your own life that reflect your walk with Christ? Are you living in a way that truly demonstrates Christ in you?

Are you in your *Judea*? Even Jesus asked His disciples, *"Who do men say that I am?"* (Matthew 16:13). Have you ever considered what people are saying about you? The good news is that you can live in such a way that people recognize you as someone who stands boldly for Christ.

Are you willing to step into your *Samaria*? Yes, there will be skeptics, critics, and even those who oppose you. But do you love them enough to share Christ with them anyway? Are you willing to serve, even when met with resistance?

The world is waiting for you to rise and take your place. *Boots On The Ground* is bringing together believers like you—men and women ready to carry the gospel of the Kingdom to the nations. Will you answer the call?

5
YOU ARE QUALIFIED

> "Now, Lord, look on their threats, <u>and grant to Your servants that with all boldness they may speak Your word</u>, "by stretching out Your hand to heal, and that signs and wonders may be done through the name of Your holy Servant Jesus." And when they had prayed, the place where they were assembled together was shaken; <u>and they were all filled with the Holy Spirit, and they spoke the word of God with boldness </u>(Acts 4:29-31).

When Peter and John were detained by the religious leaders after healing a lame man, the authorities did everything they could to intimidate them. The chief priests, the captain of the Temple, and the Sadducees threatened them, hoping to silence their message. But it didn't work. Instead, Scripture tells us that these leaders *took note* of the apostles' boldness (Acts 4:13, 19-20). That boldness wasn't just a personality trait—it was the mark of a life transformed by the Holy Spirit.

When Peter and John returned to their own company, they didn't pray for safety or favor with the authorities. They prayed for *boldness*. And God answered in a dynamic way—the place where they gathered shook, and *everyone* was filled with the Holy Spirit, speaking the Word of God with boldness.

But who was this company? They weren't the elite. They weren't religious officials. They weren't titled leaders. They were *ordinary believers*—people like you and me—empowered by the Holy Spirit to boldly proclaim the Kingdom with confidence.

This is what *Boots On The Ground* is all about: establishing, developing, and releasing believers into the fullness of their calling. The Lord's ekklesia isn't built on titles or positions but on *people*—spirit-filled, Kingdom-minded believers who are ready to step forward and make an impact.

This chapter will reveal how God is raising up a company of bold, unstoppable believers. Could you be one of them?

LET'S TALK EKKLESIA FIRST
I want to first make sure that you have a basic understanding of the ekklesia and what it is designed to do.

> ...to the intent that now the manifold wisdom of God might be made known by the [ekklesia] to the principalities and powers in the heavenly places, according to the eternal purpose which He accomplished in Christ Jesus our Lord, (Ephesians 3:10-11)

God has entrusted the demonstration of His wisdom to His Ekklesia. It is through His Ekklesia that principalities and powers in the heavenly realms will come to understand His divine plan. As the sole representative of the Kingdom of Heaven on earth, the Ekklesia stands under God's authority, and no spiritual or human force can prevail against it (Matthew 16:18).

Many Bible translations use the English word *church* in this passage, but the original Greek word is *ekklesia*. Whenever you see *church* in your Bible, remember that it refers to the *ekklesia*—the called-out assembly of believers who are empowered to carry out the will of God on earth.

Ekklesia and church are not the same. This is a foundational fact that must be understood in order to comprehend *Boots On The Ground*.

DEFINING EKKLESIA

The word *ekklesia* comes from two Greek words: "ek" (out from) and "kaleo" (to call). Together, they mean "to call out." However, *ekklesia* was never just about being called out—it was always for a specific purpose.

In the Old Testament, the idea of being called out was consistently connected to a divine assignment. By the first century, *ekklesia* had evolved beyond a general assembly; it had been adopted by Rome as a governing body. It referred to a called-out citizenry tasked with representing the interests of the Roman government in a given region.

When Jesus declared, *"I will build My ekklesia"* (Matthew 16:18), He was not referring to a religious institution but to a governing assembly. His *ekklesia* would function as Heaven's representatives on earth, carrying out the will of the Kingdom of God. Unlike the Roman *ekklesia*, which advanced the rule of Caesar, Jesus' *ekklesia* would advance the reign of God, bringing transformation to the world according to His divine purpose.

THE TRUE FOUNDATION OF THE EKKLESIA

Jesus is building His ekklesia on the revelation of who He is, not on Peter. Some religious traditions have misunderstood this truth and mistakenly teach that Jesus built His ekklesia—often mistranslated as "church"—on Peter. This error has led them to claim spiritual authority by attempting to trace their lineage back to Peter. However, Scripture makes it clear that the foundation of Jesus' ekklesia is the revelation that He is the Christ, the Son of the living God— not any human individual.

Jesus initiated this conversation by asking His disciples, "Who do people say that I, the Son of Man, am?" (Matthew 16:13). When Peter answered, "You are the Christ, the Son of the Living God" (Matthew 16:16), Jesus affirmed that this revelation of His divine identity was given by the Father (Matthew 16:17). It is on this revelation— that Jesus is the Christ, the Son of the Living God—that He is building His ekklesia. The foundation of His ekklesia is not Peter, but the truth of who Jesus is, revealed by the Father to those who believe. Let's see exactly what Jesus said to Peter.

> "You are Petros (a small stone), and on this Petra (a huge, massive, immovable rock) I will build My ekklesia." (Matthew 16:18)

The distinction in the Greek words is critical. Petros refers to a small, moveable stone, while Petra refers to a massive rock foundation. Jesus was not saying Peter was the foundation; rather, He was pointing to the revelation of His identity as the unshakable rock upon which the *ekklesia* would be built.

The fact that Jesus alone is the Rock, is shown throughout scripture. He is the chief cornerstone (Psalms 118:22; 1Corinthians 3:11). Peter even affirmed that Jesus is the Rock (1Peter 2:4-6).

Jesus did not establish His *ekklesia* on Peter but on the revelation that He is the Christ, the Son of the Living God. This foundational truth is what gives the *ekklesia* its strength, ensuring that it is built on Christ alone, not on any man.

THE EKKLESIA IS EQUIPPED WITH POWER

I want you to imagine where you are is an outpost. You have been stationed there to represent the Kingdom of Heaven. Your assignment is to establish kingdom policies in the territory. The question arises, "What tools do your have at your disposal?" "What authority do you have to carry out your assignment?"

> *And I will give you the keys of the kingdom of heaven, and whatever you bind on earth will be bound in*

> *heaven, and whatever you loose on earth will be loosed in heaven." (Matthew 16:19)*

When Jesus declared that He would build His *ekklesia*, He wasn't just forming a gathering—He was establishing a powerful, fully equipped, and divinely authorized body to represent the Kingdom of Heaven on earth!

First, He gave it the keys of the Kingdom (Matthew 16:19). That means you have access to everything you need to fulfill your God-given assignment with boldness and confidence. Nothing is lacking—every resource of Heaven is available to you!

Second, He entrusted His *ekklesia* with unmatched legislative authority. Whatever is bound or loosed in Heaven, you have the divine authorization to bind or loose the same here on earth. You are not just a bystander—you are an active participant in God's Kingdom agenda!

This is the *ekklesia*—a *called-out* assembly of Kingdom citizens, empowered to transform the world. What an incredible privilege to be part of this movement! Are you ready to step into your authority and embrace your role in the *ekklesia*? The time is now!

IS BOOTS ON THE GROUND FOR YOU?

Boots On The Ground is your launching pad into the powerful reality of the *ekklesia*. You may already sense that

God is calling you to something greater—but now it's time to take action. You are qualified to take this journey!

So, who should enlist in *Boots On The Ground*? Who will benefit the most?

1. BELIEVERS SEEKING CLARITY IN THEIR PURPOSE

    Do you feel stuck in your faith, unsure of your gifts and calling? This is for those who are ready to discover their God-given purpose and learn how to put it into action.

2. BELIEVERS WANTING TO MAKE AN IMPACT BEYOND THE CHURCH WALLS

    If you've left the traditional church system (*DONES*)[1] but still have a deep desire to serve Jesus and live out your faith in a meaningful way, *Boots On The Ground* will show you how.

3. BELIEVERS BATTLING SELF-DOUBT

    Do you feel disqualified because of past mistakes, fears, or lack of experience? You are not

---

[1] DONES are described as believers who have left the traditional church system, but seek ways to express their faith.

alone. This journey will help you see yourself the way God sees you and help you to step confidently into His plan for your life.

4. EMERGING SERVANT-LEADERS

   If you sense a call to leadership but don't know where to start, this training will equip you with the tools, confidence, and direction you need to make a Kingdom impact.

5. EVERYDAY BELIEVERS WHO UNDERSTAND THE KINGDOM

   This is not a generic category—it's for those who already understand the Kingdom but are asking, "What's next?" If you want to influence your family, community, and workplace for God's glory but need guidance on how to do it, *Boots On The Ground* is you next step.

If you see yourself in any of these categories, *Boots On The Ground* is designed for you. Are you ready to step into your Kingdom assignment? The time to move is now!

6
ESTABLISHED, DEVELOPED, AND RELEASED

The Book of Acts is a powerful historical overview of the early years of the ekklesia. Jesus had ascended back to heaven, and now the believers, lead by the apostles and prophets were navigating their way forward. They did not have a step-by-step manual, but they did have revelatory understanding of Old Testament text, and most importantly the indwelling of the Holy Ghost.

From the Day of Pentecost, I imagine everyday was a fresh new experience. People were saved, healed, and delivered from demonic oppression through the power of the risen Lord working through the believers (Acts 4:10). This, no doubt, was an exciting time to be alive. Slowly the devil began to find ways to disrupt this powerful move of God.

The religious leaders, invested in the status quo, began to harass the new believers. They arrested them, beat them, threaten them, and killed them. Yet, the believers continued to grow, turning the known religious world upside down (Acts 17:6).

A FORCED MOVE

Jesus had given clear instructions—wait for the promise of the Father, then take the message to Jerusalem, Judea, Samaria, and the ends of the earth (Acts 1:8). But instead of moving outward, the believers seemed content to stay in Jerusalem, growing in numbers but not yet stepping into the full scope of their mission.

Then, everything changed.

Sometime between one to four years after Pentecost, a fierce wave of persecution broke out. Saul, a zealous enforcer of religious law, had watched Stephen's execution and was now armed with official letters to hunt down, imprison, and even execute followers of The Way (Acts 9:1-2).

But what the enemy meant for destruction God used for expansion. Persecution forced the believers to scatter—and in scattering, they carried the gospel beyond

Jerusalem for the first time to the very places they had been instructed to go (Acts 8:1).

And as for Saul? The Lord had a divine appointment waiting for him on the road to Damascus.

> Now Saul was consenting to his death. At that time a great persecution arose against the [ekklesia] which was at Jerusalem; <u>and they were all scattered throughout the regions of Judea and Samaria, except the apostles.</u> And devout men carried Stephen to his burial, and made great lamentation over him. As for Saul, he made havoc of the [ekklesia], entering every house, and dragging off men and women, committing them to prison. <u>Therefore, those who were scattered went everywhere preaching the word.</u> (Acts 8:1-4)

I want you to focus on two key details in this narrative. First, while the believers scattered, the apostles remained in Jerusalem. Second, as they scattered, they preached the Word everywhere they went. This tells us something powerful—it wasn't just the apostles spreading the gospel, but everyday believers like you and me who carried the message of Christ into new regions. That is the point I want to emphasize.

Boots On The Ground is equipping everyday believers to take the Word beyond the four walls and into the world. When those early believers scattered, they weren't dependent on the apostles' direct oversight—they were led by the Holy Spirit's insight. This doesn't mean apostles and other ministry gifts aren't needed; rather, it reveals the divine order of God's Kingdom, where all believers can move boldly and effectively as the Holy Spirit guides them.

Now is the most opportune time to step out in faith. It took persecution to drive those first century believers into action. Most of us in the west are not facing religious persecution. We have no excuse for holding back.

HOW DOES BOOTS ON THE GROUND EQUIP BELIEVERS?

When Jesus ascended, He gave five gifts to equip the believers for the work of ministry. Apostles, Prophets, Evangelist, Pastors and Teachers have been commissioned by the Lord to bring the saints into maturity. This is a primary aspect of *Boots On The Ground*.

As the Lord showed me this work, it became obvious that many believers have been so diminished by religious systems that they don't know how to serve in the kingdom in a meaningful way. My friend Fred Tobun puts it succinctly when he says that many were born into the Kingdom, but lost in religion.[1] *Boots On The Ground* is one of

---

[1] UNLOCK THE KINGDOM IN YOU: *Discover the profound truth that you were born into the kingdom but lost in religion* © 2025 by Frederick A. Tobun Published by Restore Enterprise Limited London, England

several initiatives around the world that are working to equip the saints.

THE THREE PHASES OF BOOTS ON THE GROUND

There is a principle established in Galatians chapter 4:

> Now I say, That the heir, as long as he is a child, differeth nothing from a servant, though he be lord of all; But is under tutors and governors until the time appointed of the father. (Galatians 4:1-2)

This principle teaches us that as heirs of the Kingdom, we have full access to all its benefits. However, we must first go through a period of learning and guidance before we can fully handle what has been entrusted to us.

Galatians 4:2 reveals that this training is only temporary—there is an appointed time when the Father determines we are ready to step into our full authority. Until then, mentors and teachers help prepare us, ensuring that when the time comes, we are equipped to walk in our calling with wisdom and maturity.

This principle is the foundation of the process used in *Boots On The Ground*. The journey is structured into three key phases: Establishing, Developing, and Releasing.

Over the next few pages, you will learn how each phase works and how following these steps will strengthen your confidence while you are discovering your ministry assignment. By committing to this process, you will be equipped to move forward with clarity and purpose.

PHASE 1: ESTABLISHING

> And they continued steadfastly in the apostles' doctrine and fellowship, in the breaking of bread, and in prayers. (Acts 2:42)

The purpose of the ESTABLISHING phase is to ensure that every believer gains a solid foundation in the core doctrines of the faith and the essential principles of ekklesia. This phase also provides an opportunity to address personal lifestyle issues that could hinder spiritual growth.

1. <u>Active Participation is Absolutely Necessary</u>

    Believers grow by actively engaging in their faith. Learning happens through real-life experiences and interactions with other believers. That's why every believer should either participate in or lead a small group.

    To make small group development simple, Ekklesia Center Ministries has created Study Starters—a collection of 12-lesson study guides focused on key topics. These guides provide a structured way for believers to grow together in their understanding and application of apostolic doctrine.

2. The Power of Small Groups

   During the ESTABLISHING phase, small group gatherings play a crucial role in helping believers apply what they learn. These groups, typically made up of three to ten people, meet weekly to encourage and strengthen one another. As they interact, their 'spiritual muscles' are exercised, preparing them for greater impact in the Kingdom.

3. Becoming Committed and Intentional

   ESTABLISHING teaches you the value of commitment and intentionality. During the phase of establishing, you help to hold each other accountable to their faith walk. This serves to strengthen and build confidence in you.

4. Exploration

   It is during the ESTABLISHING phase that the Holy Spirit can begin revealing your purpose. There is power in knowing what God has designed for you.

PHASE 2: DEVELOPING

> ...but is under guardians and stewards until the time appointed by the father. (Galatians 4:2)

1. DEVELOPING is an exciting phase. It is designed for those who are actively involved in a small group.

Believers are developed as they have the opportunity to minister in a safe environment. It is during this phase that you learn how to effectively exercise your gifts.

As you navigate through the DEVELOPING phase, you will learn how to address everything you face with Kingdom values and solutions. You will learn how to function in real world situations with the power of the Holy Spirit.

2. DEVELOPING will also include identifying potential regional leadership. Elders, deacons, and five-fold ministry gifts must be nurtured and developed. In addition to in-depth training, it will require prayer and the leading of the Holy Spirit to identify these leaders (Acts 13:1-3; 20:28; Titus 1:5)

PHASE 3: RELEASING

> And they went out and preached everywhere, the Lord working with them and confirming the word through the accompanying signs. Amen. (Mark 16:20)

ESTABLISHING and DEVELOPING have no value without there being a time for RELEASING. Your gifts and calling must find a place of expression. *Boots On The Ground* is designed to prepare you. You should be free to go wherever you are led by the Holy Spirit. You will be among those who are transforming regions through the Gospel of the Kingdom.

Boots On The Ground is your first step towards serving in the Lord's ekklesia. The fact that you have this book in your hands tells me that the Lord is calling you to step out in faith and begin this journey. There is an army of believers like you being positioned to build, raise up, and repair all across this nation (Isaiah 61:4)

This can be your destiny! Let's get ready...

7
LET'S GET STARTED

What is your next step? How do you join *Boots On The Ground*? This chapter will help you get started on this powerful journey.

I pray you are as committed to the expansion of the Kingdom as I am. Just as Jesus declared,

> ...this gospel of the kingdom will be preached in all the world as a witness to all the nations, and then the end will come. (Matthew 24:14)

The message of the Kingdom is the only message for all generations. Jesus is emphatic in identifying 'this gospel of the kingdom' as distinct from all others. The end cannot come until 'this good news of the government' of God' is proclaimed in all the inhabited earth.

This is more than a proclamation, it is the demonstration of the rule, reign and authority of God. The Gospel of the Kingdom is proclaimed 'as a witness' to all the nations. Let's examine the word 'witness'.

In this passage, the Greek word 'marturion' is translated as 'witness'. Some translations use the word 'testimony'. In both instances, this word speaks of something that serves as proof or verification of a fact. This suggests that the Gospel of the Kingdom is accompanied by tangible evidence of its existence.

> "Whatever city you enter, and they receive you, eat such things as are set before you. "<u>And heal the sick there, and say to them, 'The kingdom of God has come near to you.</u>' (Luke 10:8-9)

> "If Satan also is divided against himself, how will his kingdom stand? Because you say I cast out demons by Beelzebub. "And if I cast out demons by Beelzebub, by whom do your sons cast them out? Therefore they will be your judges. "But <u>if I cast out demons with the finger of God, surely the kingdom of God has come upon you</u>. (Matthew 12:24; Luke 11:18-20)

Matthew and Luke show us that healing and deliverance are evidence of the kingdom. Another such connection of miracles and the kingdom is found in the conversation between Jesus and Nicodemus. We need to be clear as to what Nicodemus asked, and how Jesus answered him.

> There was a man of the Pharisees named Nicodemus, a ruler of the Jews. This man came to Jesus by night and said to Him, "Rabbi, we know that You are a teacher come from God; for no one can do these signs that You do unless God is with him." Jesus answered and said to him, "Most assuredly, I say to you, unless one is born again, he cannot see the kingdom of God." (John 3:1-3)

Nicodemus came to Jesus, acknowledging that the miracles He performed were undeniable evidence of God's presence. He said, *"We know... no one can do these signs unless God is with him"* (John 3:2). Implicit in what he asked Jesus was that the signs—visible and tangible manifestations—had caught their attention, sparking discussions among Nicodemus and his peers. However, rather than focusing on the miracles themselves, Jesus shifted the conversation to what Nicodemus truly needed to perceive: *the Kingdom of God.*

This distinction is critical. Jesus did not simply tell Nicodemus what to *do*—He told him what he needed to *see*. Only by seeing the Kingdom could Nicodemus understand the true source of the miracles. Later, in John 3:5, Jesus explained what was necessary to enter the Kingdom, reinforcing that these supernatural works were evidence of the Kingdom's reality on earth.

This is the foundation of *Boots On The Ground*. It is not just a concept or religious phrase—it is the demonstration of the invisible Kingdom through real, observable actions. The work we do—whether feeding the hungry, clothing the poor, or meeting practical needs—are the gateway to providing tangible evidence of God's reign. These acts are not separate from the supernatural; they are the first steps toward becoming an ekklesia, a gathering of believers manifesting God's power.

As we commit to walking in Acts 2:42—devoting ourselves to apostolic teaching, fellowship, breaking bread, and prayer—we position ourselves for greater signs and wonders to manifest.

The miracles Jesus performed were not just divine interventions; they were proof of the Kingdom's presence. Likewise, *Boots On The Ground* must be rooted in evidence-based activities that flow from the Kingdom of God, making His rule visible and undeniable in our communities.

IT'S TIME FOR YOU TO PUT BOOTS ON THE GROUND

This book was written with one goal in mind—to move you to action. Now that you have a clear understanding of *Boots On The Ground*, it's time to take the next step. As with any journey, challenges will arise, but I have prayerfully worked to remove unnecessary obstacles so you can move forward with confidence.

Recently, I had the opportunity to speak at the Ekklesia Global Roundtable, on the topic *From Vision to Mission*. It was facilitated by my friend Dayo who I mentioned in the introduction of this book. In that presentation, I outlined twelve key factors that often hold believers back from stepping out in faith to pursue ekklesia. In the next few pages, I've distilled them down to six primary challenges—more importantly, I'll show you how we plan to mitigate these barriers, so they don't hold you back.

You don't have to stay stuck in hesitation or uncertainty. The time to act is now. Let's break through what's been stopping you and step boldly into what God has called you to do.

Barrier 1: Fear of Isolation and Rejection

Ekklesia is new and emerging in seemingly isolated places around the world. Many who are learning what ekklesia is, are finding themselves alone. They worry about feeling disconnected from the community they've relied on for spiritual and emotional support. At times, leaving the church system leads to judgment or criticism from others.

No one can control how people respond to anything. Whenever one group rejects the kingdom, there are many more seeking to know more about it. Therefore, it is unproductive to attempt to convince anyone that has no interest (Matthew 10:11-14; Luke 10:3-11). True ekklesia fosters genuine relationships that build mutual encouragement and accountability.

<u>What we will do to help</u>

✓ We are building a member only BOTG Community Page on our website where you can interact with other believers around the world. This will serve as a continuous and tangible reminder that you are not alone. Access to this page is by invitation only, to ensure you are connected to like-minded individuals.

✓ We will host regular live events that will serve to train, encourage, and answer 'in real time', questions you may have.

Barrier 2: Tradition, Familiarity, Cultural, and Social Identity

Many people struggle to move into greater spiritual things because of deep emotional ties to traditions, cultural identity, and familiar practices. Humans naturally seek comfort in what they know, often associating with those who share their racial, religious, or cultural background. While these connections are not inherently wrong, they become a barrier when they take precedence over biblical truth. Jesus warned against making God's Word ineffective through human traditions (Mark 7:13), emphasizing the need to prioritize Scripture over longstanding customs.

Additionally, for many, church is deeply intertwined with their social and cultural identity, making it difficult to separate faith from tradition. However, the Bible teaches that in Christ, we become new creations (2Corinthians 5:17), meaning our primary identity should be rooted in Him rather than cultural norms.

When believers hold too tightly to tradition and social comfort, they may resist spiritual growth, missing the deeper transformation and calling that God has for them. True spiritual advancement requires letting go of anything—no matter how familiar—that hinders full obedience to God's Word.

What we will do to help you

Here's how Ekklesia Center Ministries can help you overcome this barrier and step into greater spiritual growth:

- ✓ Biblical Teaching That Transforms – At Ekklesia Center Ministries, we prioritize the Word of God over tradition. Through in-depth teaching, small group studies, and other resources, we help you break free from man-made customs that may be hindering your spiritual progress, ensuring that your faith is firmly rooted in biblical truth (Mark 7:13).

- ✓ You have free access to over 600 videos on our YouTube Channel that will help lay firm biblical foundations.

- ✓ Discovering Your Kingdom Identity – We guide believers in embracing their true identity in Christ, beyond cultural and denominational labels. Our training is designed to equip you to walk confidently in your calling, fully understanding that you are a new creation (2Corinthians 5:17).

- ✓ A Community That Encourages Growth – The BOTG Community page will connect you with people from all walks of life. Change is easier when you're surrounded by the right people.

- ✓ Ekklesia Center Ministries will help you to connect with like-minded believers through home gatherings, leadership training, and mentorship, providing the support and accountability needed to step out in faith and fully live out your Kingdom purpose.

<u>Barrier 3: Misunderstanding of Ekklesia and Doctrine</u>

In this time of transition, there are a plethora of definitions of ekklesia. Some still believe it is the Greek word for the English word church. Others reduce it to basic semantics while others try to minimize by saying it is an unnecessary topic. People often lack clarity on what ekklesia is and how it differs from the traditional church system.

> "And I say also unto thee, That thou art Peter, and upon this rock I will build my [ekklesia]; and the gates of [hades] shall not prevail against it." (Matthew 16:18)

Ekklesia and church are not the same. Ekklesia is a community of called-out believers, not a physical building or institution.

In addition to misunderstanding ekklesia, there arises questions relating to doctrine. Does ekklesia change basic doctrinal truths (i.e. salvation by grace through faith, water baptism, etc.). There is often a real and legitimate concern as to how ekklesia impacts biblical doctrine. This book cannot cover every doctrine, but this matter can be summarized in stating that no biblical doctrine is changed to fit ekklesia.

What we will do to help you

- ✓ First, we will provide you with historical, etymological, and biblical facts about ekklesia. Factual evidence will build your confidence.

- ✓ Second, we will point you to resources and encourage you to seek out resources that clarify the reality of ekklesia. What you personally discover, you are more apt to retain.

- ✓ When necessary, we will show the difference between biblical doctrines (Hebrews 6:1), and denominational preferences (Mark 7:7).

- ✓ We will teach sound doctrine that can be lived out in the believers daily walk (Titus 2:1)

Barrier 4: Leadership Conflicts

The challenge of leadership in the emerging ekklesia has two sides. On one side, there are leaders who fear losing their power and control. As ekklesia rises, they see their platform and influence threatened, leading them to resist and even fight against this movement to protect their status. This is not a new struggle. Scripture speaks of Diotrephes, who sought to have preeminence

(3John 9), and Simon the sorcerer, who built an image of greatness around himself (Acts 8:9). Then there were the religious leaders who said it plainly,

> Then many of the Jews who had come to Mary, and had seen the things Jesus did, believed in Him. But some of them went away to the Pharisees and told them the things Jesus did. Then the chief priests and the Pharisees gathered a council and said, "What shall we do? For this Man works many signs. "If we let Him alone like this, everyone will believe in Him, and the Romans will come and take away both our place and nation." (John 11:45-48)

These leaders became more focused on preserving their position than pursuing God's purpose.

On the other side, there are followers who exhibit misplaced and unquestioning loyalty to leadership. While honoring leaders is biblical, blindly following someone without discerning the truth can be dangerous. Many times, these devoted followers are used to serve a leader's personal agenda—only to be discarded when they are no longer needed. Sadly, many leaders are more concerned with their power than the purpose of God.

What we will do to help you

- ✓ We will endeavor to both teach and demonstrate true biblical leadership. True Kingdom leadership is not about power or control—it is about serving, equipping, and releasing others to fulfill God's purpose.
- ✓ As ekklesia emerges, we must seek leaders who walk in humility and who remain anchored in biblical truth above all else.
- ✓ We will teach and demonstrate how to honor leadership (1Thessalonians 5:12-13; Hebrews 13:7, 17)

Barrier 5: Religious Programs, Events, and Services

Church, as we know it today, has become a structured system for practicing religion. Across denominations, most churches follow a similar pattern, with services and routines that members can predict from week to week. This structure has become so ingrained in our thinking that until recently, few questioned whether many church practices align with Scripture.

The programs and traditions within the church system often provide both spiritual and social fulfillment, making it difficult for people to step away. Regular events offer moments of inspiration and entertainment, while weekly services follow familiar patterns. Despite denominational differences, most churches operate within the same basic framework, repeating variations of the same activities week after week, month after month, and year after year.

<u>What we will do to help you</u>

Overcoming the structured religious system requires intentional steps toward rediscovering and living out *ekklesia* as Jesus intended. Here are three key solutions:

✓ Return to Biblical Foundations

Many church traditions have been passed down without being examined against Scripture. To move beyond the religious system, believers must study the Bible with fresh eyes, focusing on how the early *ekklesia* functioned. This includes gathering in homes, sharing life together, and actively making disciples rather than simply attending services (Acts 2:42-47).

✓ Prioritize Relationship Over Routine

The church system often emphasizes structured programs over genuine relationships. To break free, believers must shift from passive attendance to active engagement—building authentic spiritual communities where people grow together, encourage one another, and operate in their God-given gifts (Ephesians 4:11-16). This means fostering environments where discipleship happens naturally through real-life interactions, not just organized events.

- ✓ Embrace Kingdom-Minded Leadership

    Many churches operate under hierarchical leadership structures that limit participation to a select few. True *ekklesia* empowers people to function in their calling without unnecessary titles or control. Leaders should equip and release people into ministry rather than simply maintain an audience (Ephesians 3:10, Matthew 28:19-20). Creating regional expressions of *ekklesia* where believers gather, pray, and minister together is key to advancing the Kingdom outside institutional constraints.

    Boots On The Ground is a model that seeks to emulate first century values and structure. By returning to biblical truth, fostering authentic relationships, and embracing a leadership model that equips rather than controls, believers can step into the fullness of *ekklesia* and expand the Kingdom of God.

Barrier 6: Comfortable, Consumer Driven Christianity

The Christian consumer mindset is one of the greatest impediments to kingdom expansion. Consumer-driven individuals often approach church (not ekklesia) with a mindset focused on personal preferences and convenience rather than a commitment to biblical discipleship. They seek to be entertained over being edified.

Here are five things consumer minded individuals seek. These are gleaned from the observation of various Christian leaders who have analyzed trends in the church as we know it.[1]

1. Entertaining Worship Experience

    They seek a church with high-energy music, professional-quality production, and a dynamic atmosphere that feels engaging and emotionally uplifting. Worship is often evaluated based on personal enjoyment rather than spiritual depth.

2. Inspiring and Motivational Preaching

    Consumer-driven individuals prefer messages that are encouraging, practical, and relevant to their daily lives. They often gravitate toward churches where the sermons are short, positive, and free from challenging or convicting topics. They are usually among those with itching ears (2Timothy 4:3-4).

3. Convenience and Comfort

    Location, service times, parking, and amenities (such as coffee stations, comfortable seating, and children services) heavily influence their decision. They want a church that fits easily into their lifestyle with minimal inconvenience.

---

[1] For more information see The Barna Group, The Pew Research Center, researchers like Josh Packard and Ashleigh Hope, Christian leaders including Francis Chan, Thom Rainer, and Dallas Willard.

4. Programs That Cater to Personal Needs

    They look for a church with ministries that serve their specific interests—whether it's a strong youth program, singles ministry, networking opportunities, or recreational activities. The focus is on how the church meets *their* needs rather than how they can serve the Kingdom.

5. Non-Confrontational Environment

    Consumer-driven people often prefer a church that avoids controversial or challenging biblical teachings. They are more comfortable in an environment that prioritizes inclusivity, avoids difficult discussions about sin and repentance, and focuses on personal well-being rather than transformation.

These prove that a person has no vision for the Kingdom Mandate (Genesis 1:28). They have little or no concept of their responsibility to 'go into all the world' (Matthew 28:19). Their 'comfort' choices contrast with the biblical model of ekklesia, which calls believers to active participation, discipleship, and Kingdom expansion rather than passive consumption.

<u>What we will do to help</u>

The time to decide is now. You are being called to something greater, and we are here to challenge, equip, and provoke you to good works (Hebrews 10:24). But ultimately, the choice is yours. No one can take this step for you. We can provide the tools, the support, and the pathway—but only you can make the commitment to move forward.

This is your moment. No more hesitation. No more waiting for the perfect time. The Kingdom is advancing, and you must decide if you will step into your calling. Here's what you need to do next—because transformation begins with action.

- ✓ Embrace the Mindset of a Disciple, Not a Spectator

    Boots On The Ground is about activating believers into their Kingdom calling. This means moving beyond just attending services to actually walking in faith and ministering to others. Instead of asking, *"What can this church offer me?"* the question becomes, *"How can I advance the Kingdom in my region?"* Through *Boots On The Ground*, you will receive tools, teaching, and support to confidently engage in ministry wherever God has placed you.

- ✓ Prioritize Community Over Programs

    Traditional church models often revolve around structured programs and events, but *Boots On The Ground* encourages intentional and consistent small group gatherings where believers can grow together. Real ekklesia happens in relational settings—just like in the Book of Acts. This movement is about doing life together, not just attending a weekly event. By being part of this community, you are stepping into something greater than a religious service—you are becoming part of a Kingdom-driven family.

✓ Focus on Kingdom Purpose, Not Personal Preferences
The goal of *Boots On The Ground* is to equip and release believers into their God-given assignments. This requires letting go of a consumer-driven mentality and stepping into purpose-driven ministry. Rather than seeking comfort, we seek transformation—impacting families, communities, and cities. Jesus called His disciples to go and make more disciples (Matthew 28:19-20), and this movement is designed to help you walk in that calling.

By committing to *Boots On The Ground*, you are choosing to engage, grow, and lead rather than just observe. Are you ready to take that step?

DON'T FEAR CHANGE
Stepping into *Boots On The Ground* can feel intimidating and uncertain.

> For God hath not given us the spirit of fear; but of power, and of love, and of a sound mind (2Timothy 1:7)

Trusting God allows you to step out in faith, even when facing change. As the founder of Ekklesia Center Ministries and the author of *Boots On The Ground*, I am committed to the expansion of the Kingdom, and will do whatever is needed to help you do your God-given part.

I will guide you through everything you need to do to get started in this wonderful ministry work. Therefore, I will make two commitments to you.

Commitment 1: You won't do Boots On The Ground alone

I have spoken to many believers who sense a calling from God. They are understanding more about ekklesia, the kingdom, and eternal purpose of God, yet no one in their area seems to have the same interest. They feel isolated and without any support.

Ekklesia Center Ministries will help to fill that void through regular live group meet-ups (Zoom or similar formats) where you will meet and interact with other believers. This may not be the perfect solution, but it is an effort to help you and to keep you encouraged. Most importantly, you will be able to ask questions and gain insights from others on this journey. You won't be alone.

Commitment 2: You will get the tools you need to succeed

Your spiritual growth is empowered when you have the right tools at your fingertips! Gathering with other believers is essential, and Ekklesia Center Ministries is dedicated to equipping you with powerful resources to make every gathering meaningful and impactful.

On our website, you'll find a collection of Study Starters—specially designed to spark deep discussions and meaningful connections. Each one includes step-by-step instructions, ensuring that every gathering strengthens your faith and helps you pour into others.

In addition to our Study Starters, you have access to a growing library of inspiring books and dynamic courses—all designed to build your faith, deepen your understanding, and equip you for success.

Whether you're looking for biblical insights, practical guidance, or tools to strengthen your spiritual walk, these resources will help you grow with confidence and purpose. Every book and course is crafted to empower you, providing you the knowledge and encouragement you need to walk boldly in your calling. Don't miss the opportunity to invest in your spiritual journey—start exploring today!

Get ready to grow, engage, and experience transformation like never before! It's time to take the next step. MAKE THE COMMITMENT!

Ekklesia Center Ministries *Boots On The Ground* will be life changing for anyone willing to commit to the journey.

Take the next step!

Go to www.TheEkklesiaCenter.org and click JOIN BOTG. Then, watch the brief video I have recorded for you.

Complete the brief questionnaire, and you are on your way. I'm praying for you and looking forward to taking this journey with you as you boldly put *BOOTS ON THE GROUND* for the kingdom!

Tips for Starting A Home or Small Group Gathering

Home and small group gatherings are the foundation for developing an effective ekklesia. This is where believers grow, encourage one another, and take real steps toward Kingdom impact. The following are eight steps that can help you organize a small gathering.

1. **Seek the Lord's Direction** – Pray for wisdom and courage to start a gathering (Ephesians 6:19). Ask the Holy Spirit to prepare the hearts for those who will join you on this journey.

2. **Commit to the Full 12 Weeks** – Before starting, make a firm commitment to complete 12 consecutive weeks of gatherings. Review your calendar and set aside uninterrupted time to ensure consistency. Each Study Starter is designed as a 12-week journey, providing solid teaching and discussion opportunities that are most effective when completed without breaks.

3. **Invite 3–7 Participants** – Invite 3 to 7 friends, family, or acquaintances, to join your gathering. While the ultimate goal is to reach the unsaved, it's best to start with a group of believers to help you gain confidence in facilitating. As you grow more comfortable, future groups can and should include unbelievers. To help guide you, get a copy of *The Believer's Handbook for New Testament Gatherings* available on *The Ekklesia Center* website. Encourage everyone you invite to commit to attending and actively participating for all 12 weeks, as growth and fellowship happens through consistency!

4. **Establish a Regular Meeting Time and Place** – As a group, agree on a specific day, time, and location for your gatherings. Decide whether to meet in your home or another suitable setting. Choose a quiet, distraction-free environment that fosters meaningful conversation, deep connection, and spiritual growth without interruption.

5. **Share a Meal Together** – Gathering around a meal is an essential part of the Acts 2:42 model, as it strengthens fellowship and deepens relationships. Each week, plan a shared meal, whether as a simple potluck or by rotating meal responsibilities among group members. Breaking bread together fosters connection and a sense of community.

6. **Select a Study Starter** – Choose a Study Starter to guide your group discussions. While there are many options available, *Living Holy* is recommended as the best starting point. This study helps participants examine their faith and encourages them to live according to biblical principles. Use the Study Starter as a guide, but allow the Holy Spirit to lead. Encourage open dialogue, personal application, and always close with prayer.

Note: Each participant should purchase and download their own Study Starter to stay engaged throughout the 12 weeks. Scan the QR code to get started!

7. **Celebrate the Lord's Table at Every Gathering.** The Lord's Table is a sacred and central part of your gatherings, aligning with the biblical pattern of Acts 2:42. As Scripture reminds us, *"For as often as you eat this bread and drink this cup, you proclaim the Lord's death till He comes."*

(1Corinthians 11:26). Each time you partake, you are not only remembering Christ's sacrifice but also declaring His victory, embracing the new covenant, and strengthening your identity as His body.

Receiving the Lord's Table together fosters a deeper sense of reverence, gratitude, and spiritual connection within your group. It serves as a time of reflection, renewal, and commitment to walk in the grace and power of Jesus Christ.

To ensure that this time is meaningful and spiritually enriching, review *'Tips for Receiving the Lord's Table in Your Home or Small Group Gathering'* in this book. These insights will help you lead with understanding and reverence, making each gathering a powerful encounter with the presence of God.

8. **Plan the next gathering** – before you dismiss your gathering, make sure that everyone is clear as to when and where the next meeting will take place. Even if you are meeting at the same place each week, it doesn't hurt to remind everyone of the day and time of the next meeting. If someone missed this gathering, as the facilitator, make sure you contact them and update them on the next day and time you will be gathering.

Consider this—your gathering could be the spark that brings Kingdom transformation to your home, community, and beyond!

To learn more, watch the 17-part Series
EKKLESIA PRINCIPLES OF GATHERING
on The Ekklesia Center's YouTube Channel
https://youtu.be/FjyopSlL_GU?si=G_k29e8p_YOd92G4

Order a copy of
The Believers Handbook for New Testament Gatherings
TheEkklesiaCenter.org/products

Notes

Tips for Receiving the Lord's Table in your Home or Small Group Gathering

The Lord's Table is a vital expression of our faith, given by Jesus for all believers to observe. It is not limited to a church building or clergy but can be shared in any gathering of believers, including homes and small groups.

This sacred act strengthens our unity in Christ, reminds us of His sacrifice, and reaffirms the covenant we have with Him. Whether you are leading or participating, every believer has the privilege and responsibility to receive communion with reverence and understanding. The following guide will help you prepare and partake in a way that honors the significance of this powerful moment.

Scripture Reference

> For I received from the Lord that which I also delivered to you: that the Lord Jesus on the same night in which He was betrayed took bread; and when He had given thanks, He broke it and said, "Take, eat; this is My body which is broken for you; do this in remembrance of Me." In the same manner He also took the cup after supper, saying, "This cup is the new covenant in My blood. This do, as often as you drink it, in remembrance of Me." For as often as you eat this bread and drink this cup, you proclaim the Lord's death till He comes. Therefore whoever eats this bread or drinks this cup of the Lord in an unworthy manner will be guilty of the body and blood of the Lord. But let a man examine himself, and so let him eat of the bread and drink of the cup. (1Corinthians 11:23-28)

How To Prepare for Communion

Before the gathering be sure you have both the 'bread' and the 'grape juice' available. Although some groups use wine, I highly recommend that non-alcoholic grape juice be used.

Using grape juice instead of wine during communion in a small group setting ensures inclusivity, practicality, and a clear focus on the spiritual significance of the Lord's Table. Grape juice allows everyone to participate, including children, individuals recovering from addiction, and those who abstain for personal or health reasons. It also prevents potential confusion among unbelievers who may be attending your gathering. It keeps the focus on the message of Christ rather than on the elements themselves.

Using grape juice eliminates the risk of distraction or misinterpretation, ensuring that communion remains a sacred act of remembrance rather than a discussion about alcohol use. Its accessibility and ease of storage make it a practical choice, while also reinforcing the understanding that all believers can facilitate the Lord's Table in a way that honors Christ and welcomes everyone into the experience.

The bread used for communion can be a small loaf that is broken into bite-sized pieces for easy sharing. Some groups choose to use pita bread or unsalted crackers as an alternative. The key is to use simple, unleavened bread that symbolizes the body of Christ, ensuring it is easily accessible for all participants.

Another alternative is to purchase a communion kit where the wafer and juice are pre-packaged. These are available at most Christian bookstores or online. Each of the following list of companies can provide you with quality communion supplies.

Kingdom.com

WCCproducts.com

Christanbook.com

LivingGraceCatalogue.com

ConcordiaSupply.com

Finally, keep the communion elements separate from the food you prepare for your group meal.

STEPS FOR RECEIVING THE LORD'S TABLE

1. Read & Reflect on 1Corinthians 11:23-28

    Encourage participants to meditate on the significance of Christ's sacrifice. One person can share what these passages mean to them.

2. Encourage everyone to examine and prepare their heart to receive communion. Take a moment for self-examination based on 1Corinthians 11:27-28. This is a perfect time for repentance.

3. Bless & Share the Bread

    Sample Prayer: Heavenly Father, we come before You as one body, united in faith and gratitude for the sacrifice of Jesus Christ. As we receive this bread, we remember His body, broken for us, that we may walk in wholeness, healing, and redemption. Thank You for Your love poured out through the cross and for the covenant of grace we share. May this bread strengthen our spirits, renew our minds, and draw us closer to You and to one another. In Jesus' name, Amen.

Pass the bread to each person, saying, "This is Christ's body, broken for you. Take and eat in remembrance of Him." The group should eat their bread together.

4. Bless & Share the Cup

    (Each participant should have their own individual cup of juice.)

    Sample Prayer: Heavenly Father, we come together in reverence and gratitude as we receive this cup, the symbol of the precious blood of Jesus Christ. Through His sacrifice, we are cleansed, redeemed, and brought into a new covenant of grace. Thank You for the forgiveness of our sins and the gift of eternal life. As we partake, may our hearts be renewed in Your love, our faith strengthened, and our lives reflect the power of Your redemption. We commit ourselves afresh to walk in unity and obedience to Your will. In Jesus' name, Amen.

    Remind the group that, "This is the new covenant in Christ's blood. Take and drink in remembrance of Him." The group should drink at the same time.

5. Give Thanks & Worship Together

    Close with thanksgiving and prayer. You may sing a worship song, share testimonies, or read from scripture.

The Study Starter Series
Powerful study guides for small groups

Study Starters are the perfect tool to ignite meaningful discussions and growth in your home or small group gathering. Each 12-week Study Starter is packed with rich content designed to equip and engage every participant, fostering deeper understanding and connection.

For the best experience, we encourage each participant to have their own copy. Simply scan the QR code to purchase and download your Study Starter today—because transformation happens when everyone is prepared and actively involved!

Visit TheEkklesiaCenter.org and click Study Starters in the navigation bar.

MORE BOOKS BY TIM KURTZ

LEAVING CHURCH BECOMING EKKLESIA: *BECAUSE JESUS NEVER SAID HE WOULD BUILD A CHURCH*

NO LONGER CHURCH AS USUAL: *RESTORING FIRST CENTURY VALUES AND STRUCTURE TO THE 21ST CENTURY CHURCH*

JESUS CHRIST SON OF THE LIVING GOD: *UNDERSTANDING THE REVELATION THAT BUILDS THE EKKLESIA*

7 FACTS WHY JESUS DIDN'T SAY HE WOULD BUILD A CHURCH *AND WHAT IT MEANS TO YOU*

DISCOVER YOUR CALLING PURPOSE AND MINISTRY *TO EXPAND THE KINGDOM OF GOD IN THE EARTH*

THE BELIEVERS GUIDE FOR NEW TESTAMENT GATHERINGS

THE BELIEVERS GUIDE FOR LEAVING CHURCH BECOMING EKKLESIA

ALL BOOKS AVAILABLE AT:

WWW.THEEKKLESIACENTER.ORG/PRODUCTS

My Notes

My Notes

My Notes

My Notes

My Notes

MORE BOOKS BY TIM KURTZ

LEAVING CHURCH BECOMING EKKLESIA: *Because Jesus never said He would build a church*

NO LONGER CHURCH AS USUAL: *Restoring First Century Values and Structure to the 21st Century Church*

JESUS CHRIST SON OF THE LIVING GOD: *Understanding the revelation that builds the ekklesia*

7 FACTS WHY JESUS DIDN'T SAY HE WOULD BUILD A CHURCH *and what it means to you*

DISCOVER YOUR CALLING PURPOSE AND MINISTRY *to expand the Kingdom of God in the earth*

THE BELIEVERS GUIDE FOR NEW TESTAMENT GATHERINGS

THE BELIEVERS GUIDE FOR LEAVING CHURCH BECOMING EKKLESIA

ALL BOOKS AVAILABLE AT:

www.TheEkklesiaCenter.org/products

www.ingramcontent.com/pod-product-compliance
Lightning Source LLC
Chambersburg PA
CBHW070450050426
42451CB00015B/3418